WITHDRAWN

D Is for Dog

Citizen Dog³
by Mark O'Hare

D1611278

**Andrews McMeel
Publishing**

Kansas City

to
me

Foreword

If dogs could read, they'd naturally read *Citizen Dog*.

Slowly, but in due time, they'd begin to realize that they are the masters while we are the slobbering, sycophantic pets, and they'd turn our lives into living hells of stupid tricks, leftover food, and having to relieve ourselves in the street, even on rainy days.

Nevertheless, the good news is that *Citizen Dog* is a true original—the freshest, funniest, most delightful new comic strip in years!

—Mell Lazarus, creator of *Momma* and *Miss Peach*

P.S. The bad news is that dogs can read.

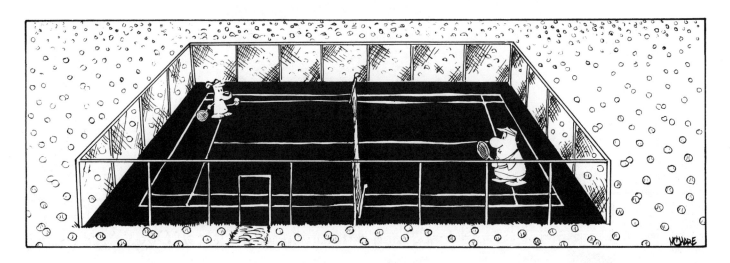

10

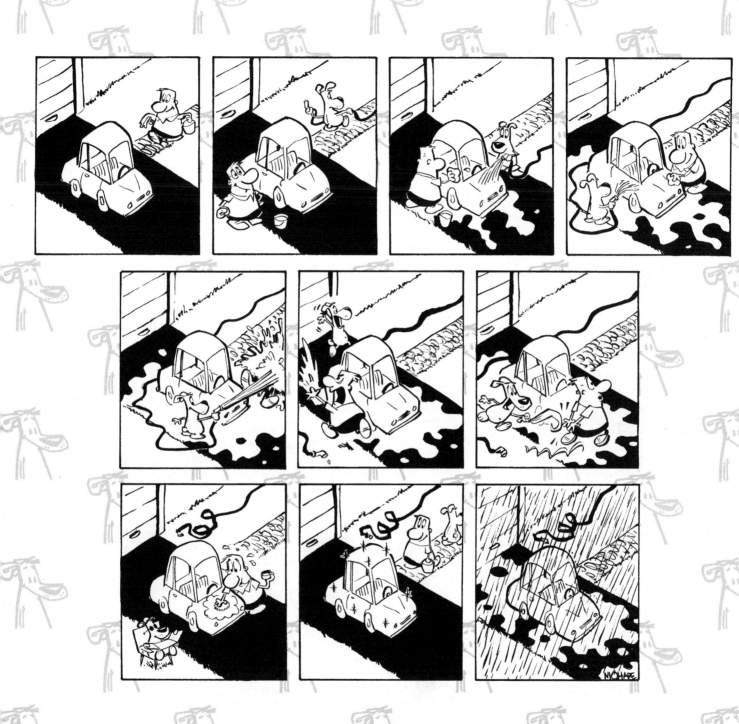

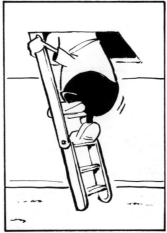

16

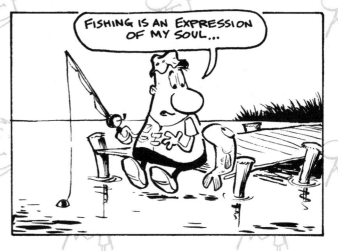

The French impressionist anxiously retreats to the only true studio he knows — NATURE!

Out here, he is free of the bondage of history and culture, free to immerse himself in the wild spontaneity of the present.

The French impressionist should remember to bring bug spray next time.

French impressionists who wait for inspiration get stood up every time.

The French impressionist finds inspiration in the collage of colors reflected from a pond of lily pads.

What secrets lie between these ripples of green and blue, beneath these shimmering pools of light and shadow.

Monet never mentioned anything about alligators.

18

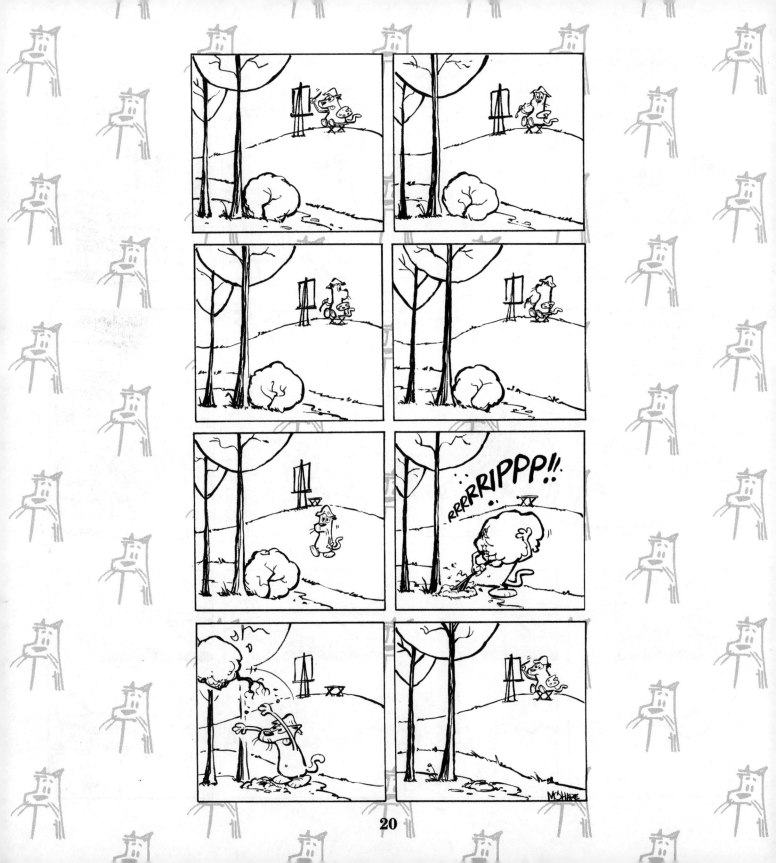

BACK TO SCHOOL ALREADY, EH?

NO MORE TRIPS TO THE POOL... TO THE BEACH....

NO MORE SUMMER CAMP....

AHHHH-HA-HA HA HA HA HA HA HA HA HA HA HA HA HA HA

I SEE IT'S GOING TO BE AN INTERESTING SCHOOL YEAR.

ARE YOU FOLLOWING ME TO SCHOOL?

YEP.

TRY NOT TO TAKE IT TOO PERSONALLY, MAGGIE. WE DO THIS TO ALL THE KIDS.

IT'S SORT OF A CANINE HAZING RITUAL.

WE'RE DOGS, MAGGIE.

IT'S WHAT WE DO.

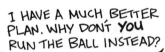

35

"FRUITY HOOPS ARE A GOOD SOURCE OF TEN ESSENTIAL VITAMINS AND MINERALS."

"COLLECT THIRTY PROOFS OF PURCHASE AND ENTER TO WIN A **FRUITY BEAR** LUNCH PAIL."

"DISTRIBUTED BY GENERAL CEREAL INC., P.O. BOX 320, BATTLE CREEK, MICHIGAN 49052."

IS IT REALLY NECESSARY TO READ **EVERY** PANEL OF THE CEREAL BOX?

"NET. WT. 13.5 OUNCES."

DO DOGS EVER HAVE TO GO TO SCHOOL?

YEAH... SOMETIMES THEY DO.

BUT THEY DON'T TEACH DOG THINGS. THEY TEACH PEOPLE THINGS.

...SO DOGS CAN BE MORE LIKE PEOPLES.

BUT ME AND ARLO HERE... WE WERE NEVER INTO THAT.

NO, MAN. WE'RE THE REAL THING.

100% ALL NATURAL DOG.

NO ARTIFICIAL ADDITIVES OR PRESERVATIVES.

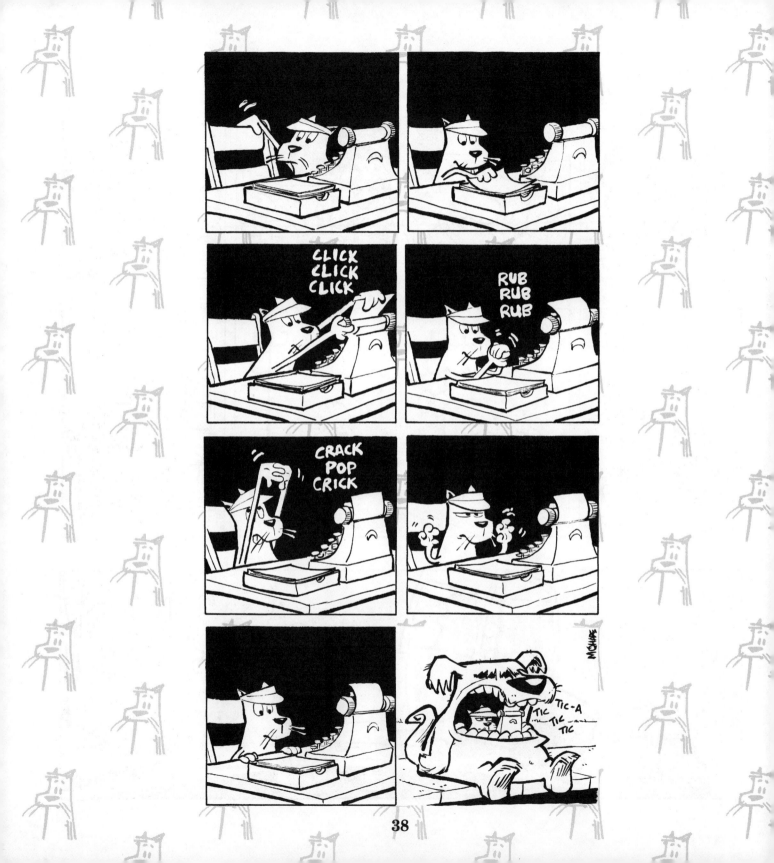

41

43

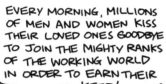

45

47

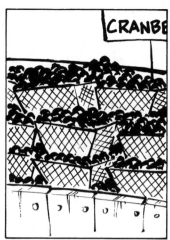

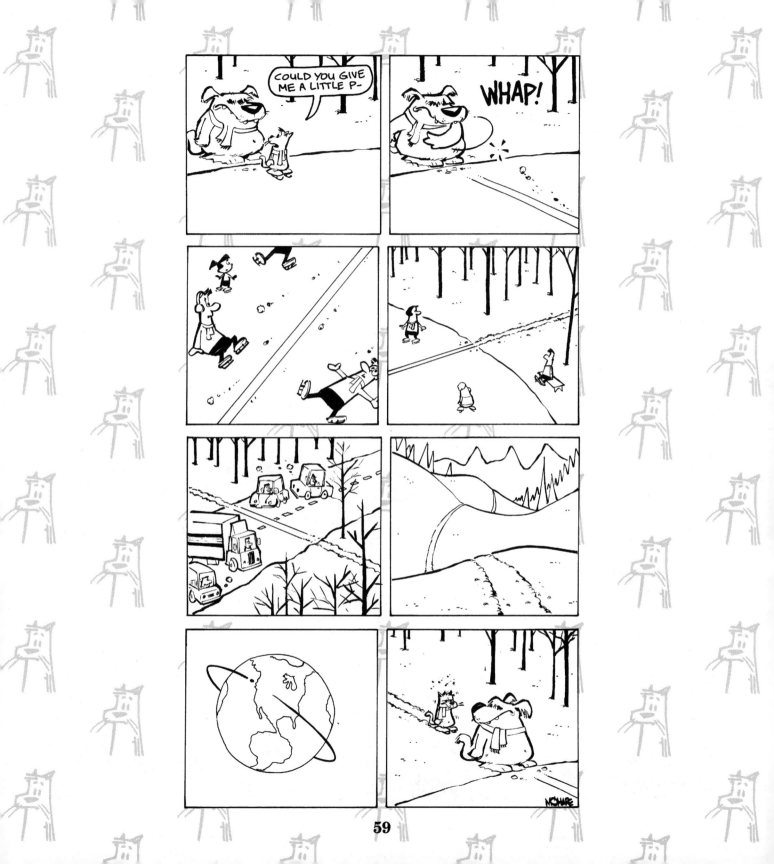

IT'S A WALLET.

WHAT'S A WALLET?

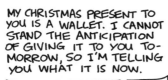

MY CHRISTMAS PRESENT TO YOU IS A WALLET. I CANNOT STAND THE ANTICIPATION OF GIVING IT TO YOU TOMORROW, SO I'M TELLING YOU WHAT IT IS NOW.

IT'S BROWN LEATHER. HERE'S THE RECEIPT IN CASE YOU DON'T LIKE IT AND WANT TO MAKE AN EXCHANGE.

EVERYONE GETS SO STRESSED OUT THIS TIME OF YEAR.

IT'S A KEY CHAIN.

SNEAKERS?

I WASN'T SURE WHAT TO GET YOU. DO CATS WEAR SNEAKERS?

SURE. WHAT THE HECK.

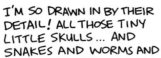

OAK TREE ELEMENTARY

YOU KNOW, I'M NOT GOING DIRECTLY HOME FROM SCHOOL TODAY.

THAT'S OK.

I HAVE TO STUDY AT THE STUPID, BORING OL' LIBRARY. I'M SURE YOU DON'T WANT TO COME IN.

I DON'T MIND.

I'LL PROBABLY BE IN HERE FOR HOURS. YOU SHOULD JUST GO ON WITHOUT ME.

I GOT NOTHIN' BUT TIME.

FLICK!

THE LIBRARY SHOULD HAVE A SNACK BAR.

THEY COULD PUT IT IN THE REFERENCE SECTION... SOMETHING QUAINT WHERE FOLKS COULD CHIT-CHAT OVER A BAGEL AND A HOT MOCHA AND LISTEN TO SOME JAZZ.

NOW THAT WOULD LIVEN UP THE JOINT A BIT. IT'S WAY TOO QUIET IN HERE.

IT'S A LIBRARY!!!

THEY COULD EVEN KNOCK OUT THE WORLD HISTORY SECTION AND SQUEEZE IN A FEW BOOTHS.

CRUNCH CRUNCH MUNCH MU
UNCH CRUNCHY MUNCH MUNCH
H KA-CRUNCHY CRUNCH CRUNCH C
MUNCH MU

77

WE INTERRUPT OUR REGULARLY SCHEDULED COMIC STRIP TO BRING YOU THIS

CDN SPECIAL REPORT

GOOD AFTERNOON, ALL. **THIS JUST IN**. ACCORDING TO VARIOUS SOURCES, SPRING HAS APPARENTLY ARRIVED. I REPEAT. SPRING IS HERE.

LET'S GO TO CUDDLES THE CAT WHO IS STANDING BY **LIVE** WHERE THE STORY IS UNFOLDING AS WE SPEAK.

THIS IS CUDDLES THE CAT COMING TO YOU **LIVE** FROM THE MOMENT WHEN SPRING HAS FINALLY ARRIVED!

SO... FLUFFY. HOW DOES IT FEEL?

IT FEELS GREAT, CUDDLES! IT'S HARD TO BELIEVE IT'S FINALLY HERE!

YOU KNOW, IT'S BEEN SUCH A LONG, HARD WINTER FOR US CATS, AND THERE WERE A LOT OF TIMES WHEN WE WEREN'T SURE WE WERE GOING TO MAKE IT. BUT WE PULLED TOGETHER AND WORKED REALLY HARD AND WE DID IT!

WELL, THERE YOU HAVE IT. **SPRING HAS OFFICIALLY ARRIVED!** BACK TO YOU, MEL!

WOOOO!

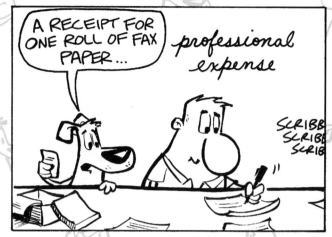

DESPITE THEIR VALIANT ALL-WEEKEND ATTEMPT TO CLEAN OUT THE GARAGE, THE ONLY MEMENTOS THAT FERGUS AND MEL WERE SUCCESSFULLY ABLE TO SEPARATE THEMSELVES FROM EMOTIONALLY WERE A TIKI LAMP, THREE PAIRS OF JEANS AND A MASON JAR.

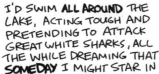

WHY DO YOU SPEND SO MUCH TIME ON THAT THING?

I'M PARTICIPATING IN WHAT WE CALL THE "GLOBAL VILLAGE."

USING THE INTERNET, I CAN COMMUNICATE WITH PEOPLE ALL OVER THE WORLD!

I CAN TALK TO PEOPLE IN RUSSIA, JAPAN... EVEN AFRICA!

WOW!

... I CAN EVEN TALK TO DOGS IN AFRICA!

WOW!

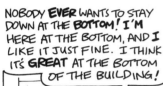

103

A "FLUFFY THE CAT" UPDATE

THE MANAGEMENT OF MUCKITY-MUCK CARTOONS APOLOGIZES FOR LEAVING OUR READERS IN SUSPENSE ABOUT THE TRAGIC FATE OF THIS MUCH LOVED AND ADMIRED CHARACTER.

THE LAST WE SAW FLUFFY, HE WAS ON A PERILOUS ASSIGNMENT IN UPPER MONGOLIA, COLLECTING FELINE DATA FOR THE CYBERCAT NETWORK.

WE ARE HAPPY TO REPORT THAT FLUFFY WAS RESCUED FROM THAT UNSETTLING SITUATION...

...AND IS CURRENTLY ON SABBATICAL ENJOYING A TASTY, ESPRESSO IN A FINE LITTLE CAFÉ IN THE FIFTH ARRONDISSEMENT, PARIS, FRANCE.

IT'S A CARTOON. WE CAN DO THINGS LIKE THAT.

BLOOP!

BORN FREEEEE...

WHERE'S MEL?

HE SENT ME TO TELL YOU THAT HE CAN'T BE HERE TO CATCH AND EAT YOU TODAY.

BUMMER.

NO, ...WAIT. I MEAN THAT'S **GREAT** ... UHHH...

I'M SO CONFUSED...

JOIN THE CLUB.

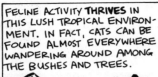

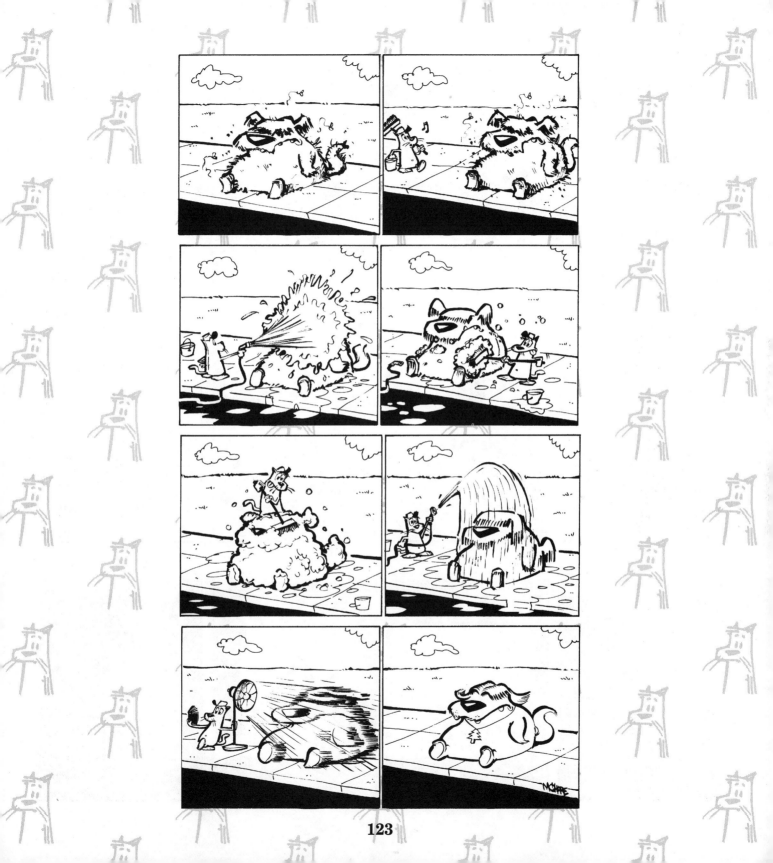

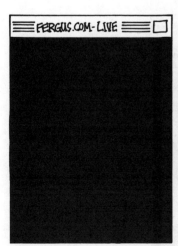

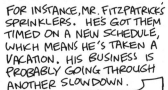